Author Platform: How to Market Books

Sell more Ebooks Online and Offline using the latest Book Marketing Tools

By Lucinda Sue Crosby and Laura Dobbins

LucyCinda 2016

Printed in USA

ISBN: 978-0-9960898-8-3

Printed in the US

LuckyCinda
www.luckycinda.com
kindlefreebies@yahoo.com

Book Design: Laura Dobbins

Disclaimer
There are no guarantees that you will make any money using the ideas and tips within this book. Since it is so dependent on genre, customer wants and your own marketing plans, how many books you sell cannot be specified. But if you work hard and apply these methods, you should see some profit increase with your books.

Table of Contents

4

Author Platform: How to Market Books

Sell more Ebooks Online and Offline using the latest Book Marketing Tools

Introduction

Ok, you've written and published a book and printed a 100 or even 1,000 copies (you optimist YOU), now what?

We have discovered that the single biggest mistake many new authors make is assuming that selling books will be a snap. After all, isn't your work better than the other 3 million plus titles already in circulation?

Six months later, the giant cobwebs on the book boxes in your garage will demonstrate how naive that assumption was.

The second misconception about promoting and selling self-published books is thinking yours will become a bestseller if you can just find someone who'll do the work for you, usually for an outlandish up-front fee. While it's true that money is helpful in getting the word out, selling enough copies to recover the outlay for publishing, distributing and marketing isn't automatic by any means. So, why bother?

The book business is like any other business: you need a game plan, a budget and a realistic set of goals. The same amount of time, money, research and preparation you took to write your book should also be dedicated to marketing your book. Of course, having a marketing proposal in place prior to launching a project is best but it's never too late and there's never been more opportunity for indie authors to succeed than now.

"More than 1,080 indie authors, most of them brand new debuts from the last five years, are currently earning $50,000 a year or more from their

Amazon sales," as noted in an in-depth analysis by AuthorsEarning.com.

In the same report, data shows some independent writers making six figures or more. (http://authorearnings.com/report/may-2016-report/)

While most of the success has been through online sales – with Amazon still king – more opportunities to break into traditional retail channels have been open for non-conventional published authors. One such example, is the recent sale of Perseu's author and distribution services to Ingram Content Group.(http://www.ingramcontent.com/)

It comes down to what your personal goals are as a writer, if you want to pen one book and see it in print whether it sells or not or if you want to make a living as an author. If the latter is you, then you will want to write great books, many of them and then find ways to reach readers.

To help you, we have written this step-by-step guide to assist you with your marketing navigation.

And whether you're new to the business or starting over in a more tech-driven world, don't be discouraged ... help is on the way!

In the following pages, you will find a variety of proven promotion strategies from simple cost-effective practices to some advanced techniques that include both online and offline possibilities.

· New book promotion ideas for 2017 and beyond
· Learn how to sell books on Amazon, Goodreads and Smashwords
· Tips on how to get into bookstores and libraries
· How to use Amazon and other digital platforms to promote ebooks
· Bonus Chapter on how to market books offline

Here's to your success and feel free to visit our site for free and paid book promotions:

Kindle Book Promos - **http://kindlebookpromos.luckycinda.com**

Let's get started.

Quick Overview and Analysis of the Book Business

Chapter 1:
An Overview of the Basics

Yes, you've heard it a 100 times but it is STILL worth repeating – the necessities for "Bestseller" status are: Title, Content, Design and Selling Strategy. Let's take a brief look at each step.

Title – When possible use names and phrases people are searching

We admit this is easier to accomplish in nonfiction but it's not impossible with fiction and certainly worthwhile. For example we published an ebook marketing guide we titled: *Sell more Ebooks – How to increase sales and Amazon rankings using Kindle Direct Publishing.*

· There are 4 key phrases in this heading that readers – mostly other authors in this case – search for on Google and Amazon: "Sell more Ebooks," "How to increase sales," How to increase Amazon rankings," and "Kindle Direct Publishing."
· The reader gets a sense of what the book is about

Other tips for choosing a compelling title:
· Keep your title as short as possible and to the point
· One-line phrases work beautifully. What is your book really about? Synthesize your answer into a tight group of words that would grab your attention, make you curious and entice you to investigate further.

Content – Determine what you want to Communicate and Why
Write what you know –

a. Are you a web designer? You can write a variety of books on this topic like: How to use basic html to make your website pop; Web Design made easy; Best Templates for Web Building ... and the list goes on.

b. Writing fiction? If you're lucky, you'll have quirky, dashing or infamous relatives with fascinating backgrounds you can feature as main or title characters. Use their stories, mannerisms, relationships and life experiences and then embellish a little or a lot – but don't skimp on accuracy of time, place and setting. Paying attention to historical and geographical details will help lure your reader into the universe you have created.

Quality matters

a. **Professional Editing**: Accidental grammar errors, misplaced punctuation, and unintentionally misspelled words will all bounce a reader right out of the text, no matter how poetic or life-altering. The money you spend on professional help – an editor, a copy editor and a proof reader – is the soundest investment you can make in your product.

b. **Design** – Looking GOOD!
First impressions matter to consumers, even more so online than on a book shelf at a store, because you can rarely scan or read through a book online.

c. **Format to E-books**

Proper formatting is a must. If you don't do it WELL, pay someone. Amazon provides a long list of ebook converting services: http://bit.ly/19ymFKP.

Fiverr is a great service to seek professional help for $5 but don't just hire the first service you see. Look at the person's rankings, customer remarks and service delivery times.(https://www.fiverr.com/)

The easiest method is to create the original text-only document in Microsoft Word and then convert it using free conversion software. Please check out the following sites:

· http://ebook.online-convert.com/convert-to-epub
· http://www.epubconverter.org/

#ew : Amazon KDP Select has added a number of tools in the past few months to aid authors with their book publishing experience. Amazon KDP now offers plugins, ebook conversion tools and epub creator. http://bit.ly/1dmo7Mj

Budgeting - No matter what you publish, you need to have some idea how you will promote it. If you have extra income and can hire an expert, more power to you. However, most writers don't have enough disposable income to go that route - or know who to trust with their labors of love.

So ...

· The basics – Budget, Time, Platforms

Advanced techniques – Keywords, Categories, Book Descriptions, Online publicity

a. **Budget**

ISB# : Some initial costs for your book include obtaining an ISBN. Bookstores require an International Standard Book Number (ISBN). This will identify your work's publisher and allow you to sell books to retailers, libraries and bookstores. An ISBN costs $125 each or bundles of 10 for $295. You can also obtain an ISBN for $55 if you are going to sell directly to consumers instead of through stores and libraries.

Library of Congress/Copyright: Obtaining a Library of Congress number is free but you will have to pay postage to send your finished product and it will cost $45 to secure the actual copyright. Although some printing companies will obtain these numbers for you, you'll still be responsible for processing fees.

Printing: Whether you print your books using Print on Demand (from one to 100 books at a time) or go traditional (in bundles of 200 or more), it will come out of your pocket. If you do plan on selling print versions of your title, remember to include distribution, storage and shipping costs. Frankly, that's what makes POD attractive – no overhead.

Keep in mind that major retailers don't like POD because it generally indicates an INDY author, which is still frowned upon by some of the major players. POD also interferes with traditional buy-back policies, an agreement between publishers, distributors and retailers. For now, let's just keep it simple.

b. Other costs:
· **Website**: If you plan on having a blog or website, which we highly recommend, you will need to consider domain registration and hosting costs. You can learn more about these online. GoDaddy.com, Hostgator.com and Wordpress.com are three popular sites.

· **Travel**: Some expenses authors often forget to include in their money plans are travel, lodging and food. If you plan on attending book signings, seminars or other events, be sure to allow for line items in your budget.

· **Advertising**: Even if your plan is for digital sales only, you will need to advertise above and beyond posting to your own website. While most advertising on digital book publicity sites is inexpensive, it will add up. NOTE: Most of these fees will cover one-day only ads.

· **Outsourcing**: Article writing and blogging are free but if you don't have the time it takes to manage these functions, you'll want to pay someone to do it.
Eventually, you can invest in software that can streamline some of these tasks.

· **Miscellaneous**: Don't forget flyers, business cards, book giveaways, press kits, postage and traditional advertising in print, radio and other media.

As you can see, forging ahead without a plan could be a costly mistake. Thoroughly vetting so-called promotional experts will protect you from investing time and money with people that can't or won't deliver. Do the homework!

But it isn't enough to have a great story, book design or appealing product price. Today's authors need to market their work even before it's made available to the public. And ideally, you want your book title, description and website to use keywords that will drive traffic to you. Even choosing book categories will determine how people find you.

Keywords and How to Use Them

Potential customers find and purchase products through identifiable and predictable code phrases because that's how internet search engines are designed ... to match a specific request with a specific result. Keywords are powerful tools for assisting internet surfers to find and purchase any product in general and your book in particular. Carefully chosen keywords, therefore, should be included when creating your headlines and book descriptions.

The #uts and Bolts of Keywords

Search engines operate on three types of software, Spider, Index and Query, that work together to collect, analyze and index web pages. Only after a web surfer enters words or a phrase in the search box is the collective information collated and made available. Over time, marketing gurus can determine which keywords people are using most for any particular product or service.

So what does that mean for authors?

It means you need to find out what people are looking for online and then find a way to position your book on the appropriate "first search pages" of Google and Amazon. If your book is consistently buried on the third page of results or lower, it will be difficult for you to compete.

Using keywords in your Book Descriptions

Whenever it makes sense, keywords should be incorporated into your book title. While it's not difficult to use traffic-driving terms or phrases in non-fiction headings, you may wish to add a subtitle to plug in necessary wordage for fiction.

Whenever you can use keywords in your online forums do so. For example, on Amazon you are allowed 7 keywords in your Digital Book setup page. On your websites you can use keywords in your headings, content and any Search Engine Optimization, (in simple terms, using words, heading and content to make your sites easy to find by people searching for your type of information online).

Tip: Make book descriptions enticing. You want to grab the reader in a few words and leaving them with wanting more. Use keywords but make the content conversational, don't just plug words in detracting potential buyers from the plot you are pitching.

The Author Marketing Club has conducted a lengthy study on book descriptions and found that books with "robust," "colorful," and "engaging" accounts can sell up to 15 percent more books than those that don't.

#ot e: AMC - The Author Marketing Club is a service of Digital Book Launch, a company owned by Internet entrepreneur and best-selling author Jim F. Kukral. It is a great site with free and paid promotional services for authors. We are premium members as well as affiliates and highly recommend these services.
(http://authormarketingclub.com/members/free-ebook-signup/)

Now that we have reviewed the basics let's learn how to put it all together to sell books.

Chapter 2:
New Publishing Trends for
Indie Authors in 2017 and Beyond

As non-traditional publishing moves past its infancy and muscles its way into adulthood, the book world continues to evolve. Technology has made it possible for writers outside of Big 5 publishing to become successful published authors – many equaling or exceeding industry-induced sales. This has forced the top players – Penguin Random House, Simon & Schuster, HarperCollins, Macmillan and Hachette – to take a second look at authors they once disdained, a vigorous shake-up of the status quo. There's good reason for this trend.

Take a look at Amazon's top 10 best-selling list on the Kindle Store. The Big 5 publishers don't make the list. Instead the top 10 are indie publishers and Amazon imprints. Here's an in-depth analyzes as posted by AuthorEarnings.

(http://authorearnings.com/report/february-2016-author-earnings-report/)

As of January 10, 2016:
· 4 of Amazon's overall Top 10 Best Selling ebooks were self-published indie titles
· 10 of Amazon's overall Top 20 Best Selling ebooks were self-published indie titles
· 56 of Amazon's overall Top 100 Best Selling ebooks — more than half — were self-published indie titles

· 20 of Amazon's overall Top 100 Best Selling ebooks were indie titles priced between $2.99 and $5.99.

As of May 2016:
· 1,340 authors are earning $100,000/year or more from Amazon sales but half of them are Indies and Amazon-imprint authors. The majority of the remainder? They come from traditional publishing's longest-tenured "old guard."
· Fewer than 115 Big Five-published authors and only 45 small- or medium-publisher authors who debuted in the past five years are currently earning $100K/year from Amazon sales. And among indie authors of the same tenure, more than 425 of them are now at a six-figure run rate.
SEE:
http://authorearnings.com/report/february-2016-author-earnings-report/

These success stories haven't gone unnoticed because although the Big 5 still won't publically embrace Indie authors, they don't shy away from signing upstart money makers to their firms.

Amanda Hocking wrote and self-published 17 e-books selling more than a million copies. This so impressed St. Martin Press, they offered Hocking a two million dollar deal for the rights to her first three books along with an exclusive for an additional four-book series.

E L James first created a following on her website for her fan fiction. Then, through a small Australian company, she self-published a little something called Fifty Shades of Grey ... the rest as they say was history. Now an international bestseller, followed by a hit film, Fifty Shades became so popular that Vintage Books scooped up rights for an attendant trilogy, which has sold more than 70 million worldwide.

Not too long ago, self-publishing was a last resort. Now, the rise of e-books and print-on-demand popularity has created never before seen opportunities and it was Amazon that blew open the doors to independent and small-press entrepreneurs; currently there are 3.2 million Kindle editions available on Amazon.

Interestingly, over the past five years, reader preferences have boomeranged. In the onset of the e-book craze, the popularity of IPads, Kindles, Nooks and other digital reading devices forced big-name brick and mortar stores like Borders and Barnes & Noble to downsize or close altogether. But in the past 18 months, research tells us that paperbacks have been making a comeback. A healthy percentage of avid readers actually prefer snuggling in bed with a good book. And according to Nielsen BookScan, expert trackers of who is buying what, college students prefer hardback text books in which they can make notations and highlight or dog-ear important subject matter.

For authors, these statistics point to a variety of options. In fact, you could actually self-publish one book while pitching a different manuscript to agents and Big 5 publishers. In this arena, like so many others, knowledge is power ... so let's investigate further:

Why self-publish?
· You can't be forced to rewrite your manuscript and you'll never have to work with an editor you don't like.
· You have full control over content, design and cover.
· You publish when you're ready.
· You retain 100-percent of your profits.
· You schedule your own speaking gigs.
· You build your own marketing plan.

The downside:
· You self-fund.
· You have no name recognition or distribution connections to get into book stores.
· You may not have the artistic or technological skills to edit, design or create book covers.
· You haven't a clue how to market your book.
· You can spend hundreds of hours and thousands of dollars on your product, building a web site and selling your work with no guarantee you'll recoup the investment.

Traditional publishing's advantages:
· The author receives $ in advance (advances, BTW, are much smaller than ever before).
· Editing, designing and marketing are funded by the publisher.
· Book signings and tours are usually scheduled and subsidized by the publisher.

Traditional publishing's major disadvantages:
· Unknown authors have little control over the final product.
· Profits are smaller because fees and costs are recovered by the agent and publisher before any royalties are dispersed.
· If a book doesn't sell well immediately, the publisher may absorb the loss and move on. They can probably afford to … can you?
· The author may have to buy back books that were printed but not sold. This eats into – and sometimes erases – the initial advance.
· It can take 3 to 5 years after signing for a book to be released.

So … what if you could secure the best of both worlds?
Hybrid publishing is an emerging concept combining elements of self-publishing and traditional publishing. This approach benefits

both publishers and authors because the structure of the deal can be tailored to meet the needs of both parties.

Say for example you're already an established Indie writer with a following. If you team with a hybrid publisher, you can negotiate to keep up to 80 percent of your digital sales and even a higher hard copy sales profit than the 7 to 10 percent offered by traditional presses. This is because the hybrid publisher and the author team up on marketing and distribution costs and responsibilities.

You should be aware that some companies work on a 50-50 basis with the author, splitting the costs of editing, designing and marketing while other companies charge a pay-per-service fee. So before you add your signature to any contract, decide what your goals are, how much you want to invest and whether the company you sign with is more apt to help you or rip you off.

Here's an outline of questions to ask, as posted at *Publishers Weekly* by Jane Freidman, the former publisher of *Writer's Digest*.
· Ask about printing runs and costs.
· Is there a sales team?
· What about distribution?
· What combinations of editing, designing and marketing packages are available and exactly who pays what?
· Speak to other authors represented by the company to investigate customer satisfaction.

While hybrid publishing is trending, it isn't a new idea. Traditional publishers have been cutting deals with authors for years. An August 2016 *Writer's Digest* article posted an in-depth look at four kinds of hybrid publishing. The blog was written by Brooke Warner, publisher of *She Writes Press* – a pay-per-service company that specializes in both traditional and new concept publishing. She also sits on the board of the Independent Book Publishers Association, (IBPA).

Here's a summary of her advice:

Hybrid publishing makes sense because it can help authors with distribution and marketing. Some hybrid companies have been formed by one-time literary agents and publishers, industry experts now using their skills to assist new authors. SEE:

http://www.writersdigest.com/online-editor/what-is-hybrid-publishing-here-are-4-things-you-should-know

Remember to research and ask questions before committing to any agreement.

Here's a small list of Hybrid Publishers to get you started.

· **Archway Publishing** – a Simon and Shuster imprint offering a variety of services including publishing and marketing packages.
(http://www.archwaypublishing.com/Default.aspx)

· **Christopher Matthews Publishing** – a Hybrid publisher offering a variety of pay-per-service deals.
(http://christophermatthewspub.com/)

· **Diversion Books** - Independent publisher based in New York City, combining decades of traditional experience with new, innovative publishing strategies. Also publishes eBook titles in collaboration with The Associated Press, Science News, and The Washington Post.
(http://www.diversionbooks.com/about)

· **Entangled Publishing** - An independent publisher of romantic fiction including YA novels offering production, distribution and marketing for its authors.
(http://entangledpublishing.com/)

· **MillCity Press** – A pay-for-service publisher offering a variety of author and publishing packages. (http://entangledpublishing.com/)

· **Soaring Eagle Books** – publishing and marketing services. (http://soaringeaglebooks.org/)

You might also take a look at the following two companies that offer legal consultation regarding book contracts or agent agreements as well as production, distribution and marketing formats.
· Dystel and Goderich Literary Management
(http://www.dystel.com/blog/)
· Writer's House
(http://www.writershouse.com/)

Physical book sales are on the rise

E-publishing is the cheapest way to get your work into the hands of readers – especially if selling on Amazon. But authors should consider setting aside a budget for print copies. Book selling outlets that report Nielsen BookScan sold 632 million books in 2015 with unit sales of print books up 5.3 percent since 2013.

This was great news for bookstores which have seen declined sales due to the digital boon online. Large retailers like Borders had to close its doors and Barnes and Noble is currently revamping floor plans for new ventures called "Concept Stores." In the next two years the book retailer is considering bigger restaurants and event venues where beer and wine will be sold. Book sections will become smaller. The expected result is that consumers will linger longer, less-known authors will get more visibility and events will draw more customers.

It is difficult to know what the next buying trend will be but authors should be ready to capitalize. For instance, one reason for increased book sales in 2015 was the popularity of adult coloring books, such as *Lost Ocean* by *The Secret Garden* illustrator Johanna Basford, as well as *The Complete Alice*, the 150th anniversary edition of Lewis Carroll's famous fairytale.

Harper Lee's second novel, *Go Set a Watchman* saw big hardback sales as did *The Girl on the Train* and EL James's *Fifty Shades of Grey* series. Ergo, writers should be prepared to offer their work in all forms.

Keep in mind that getting your book on a store shelf doesn't guarantee sales. People still need to know about your title and be intrigued enough to buy it.

Other points to ponder:

· Brick and Mortar book stores will demand at least a 40 percent discount on your sales price. So if your book retails for $10, you will need to part with it for $4. Booksellers that have upfront costs to worry about need to build in a profit – especially when they're taking a chance on an unknown writer.

· Most retailers insist on the options to purchase in bulk and to return unsold books. Without a distributor or wholesaler taking responsibility for these terms, you will have to do it yourself. And unless you already have a relationship with the store owners, it will be very difficult and expensive to do this on your own.

This is where some hybrid publishers can help.

You should also consider upfront print costs. Most publishers of any type will want 500 copies to start, an investment that will dip into any eventual profits. You can see why many authors choose to digitally produce or opt for print-on-demand – books are only produced when purchased.

POD – a look at the top 3

Print-on-Demand will continue to be an inexpensive option especially for writers choosing to go solo. If you don't have to pay someone to write, edit, design, or market your book, choosing a POD company like Createspace will be your cheapest route. If you are seeking a wider distribution or an audience outside of Amazon, Lightning Source and IngramSpark are better choices.

The above POD companies also offer distribution services to wholesalers who make titles available to book stores. Lightning Source and IngramSpark are owned by Ingram which is one of the largest world-wide wholesalers. Createspace, owned by Amazon, lists books on their sites for a fee of $25 per title and will also make your book available to Ingram.

What to consider:
· Book Binding options
· Printing Costs
· Color Options
· Set-up and listing fees

You might want to read an in-depth analysis and cost breakdown written by author Kimberly Martin at Jera Publishing. http://www.self-pub.net/blog/lightning-source-createspace-and-ingram-spark/

What about libraries?

Tight budgets have forced reduced book purchases at libraries. But with the revolution of electronic reads, libraries are adding to their digital stockpiles. Two companies that will list your titles on e-catalogues are OverDrive and Smashwords.

As you can see, the electronic age will continue to expand the ways by which authors reach readers. How you keep abreast of new technology and adapt will determine your success. Even if you pay others for your book services, you need to have an overall understanding of the whole process or you could lose your shirt. Knowledge and a plan will prevent unnecessary heartache.

Final thoughts: Joining organizations with a variety of vetted author resources is a smart way to go. Research each one to see what will best fit your needs.

Here's a list of organizations we have used or are officially affiliated with – meaning if you make a membership purchase, at no additional cost to you, Luckycinda will receive a small compensation.

· **Alliance of Independent Authors**
(https://www.allianceindependentauthors.org/)

· **American Book Sellers Association**
(http://www.bookweb.org/join)

· **Author Marketing Club**
(http://authormarketingclub.com/)

· **Independent Book Publishers Association**
(http://authormarketingclub.com/)

Book Marketing
How to get started
and which sites work best

Chapter 3:
You need a Website
to Market Books Online

No matter what other investments you make of precious time and money, you MUST have a website. The various platforms that support your book sales, such as Amazon, Barnes and Noble and Smashwords, allow you to list your profile, book descriptions and other general information. But you still need a place to make a connection with your audience of online readers and potential customers.

**Before building a website, you will have
to purchase a domain and a web host.**

Domain – This will be the name of your website. Consider using a book title or personal name. And depending on your niche, any service you may provide or info about future book projects, you could make your website even more market-friendly by using a "key word" or "key phrase." For example, if you are a writer of mystery books, you should use the word "mystery" in your website title:
· www.mysterynovels.com
· www.newmystery.com
· www.mystertrilogies.com

Web Hosting – When you build a website, you will need a place that stores all your files and a service that makes your information accessible on the Internet. There are a number of companies that offer these services at reasonable prices.

GoDaddy

Hostgator

SPECIAL #OTE: There are free web hosting services available but, in our opinion, their disadvantages far outweigh the few dollars a month you might save. As an example, with free web hosting, you don't get your own domain name, you'll probably have third party advertisements displayed on your site and the pages can be slow to upload or disappear altogether.

Website – Once you have a domain name and web host, you will need to build your website. Not nearly as complicated as it used to be, this streamlined process now usually includes ready-made templates and step-by-step instructions. For technophobes, you can always pay someone to build your website, a service offered by your webhost.

TIP: Content is key. Posting interesting information and conversational topics will draw more people to your site than advertising alone. From a promotional stance, "key words," and "key phrases," should be used in headlines, topic headings and elsewhere throughout your content because they will help guide people who are already interested in your topic in your direction. Because this subject is complex, we go into more detail on page XX. Most simply put, if you are writing about ROMANCE, you will want to use terms on your website associated with ROMANCE.

Some key phrases might be:

Romance

Romantic novels on Kindle

Love stories

Historic romance novels

How do I use my Website to make Book Sales?

Most authors are not sales savvy by nature, so understanding the pros and cons of the differing methods of selling product may take some education. It certainly did for us! One year at the Los Angeles Book Fair, we paid a large sum of money for a small space amid several other authors. Dozens of big-name publishers and television celebrities also attended the weekend event, all hawking their latest titles. Unfortunately, we discovered that about half of the possible "customers" strolling by our booth were actually other authors passing out flyers and business cards about their own books!

We soon realized too many writers (like us) don't know who to contact or where to distribute their material so they attend book festivals or (even worse) library events. Believe it: this isn't how you make sizable sales.

The same concept obtains online. Most authors don't know how to use their websites for promotion. Having to learn about blogs, marketing and social forums is time consuming and can quickly become overwhelming. But in today's digital world, a familiarity with online basics is a must.

For Do-it-Yourself authors or those new to online business, we'll keep it simple.

Website basics
· Appropriate and catchy domain name
· A design that's easy to navigate
· A clear and properly sized image of your book cover with a descriptive blurb about the story
· A short biography about you along with at least one recent, flattering photograph
· Make sure to include a payment process for purchases – like a Paypal button or link
· Contact info page

Now let's take a look at enhancing your site to attract additional readers and sales.

First, decide who you want to target. Who is your audience? Nonfiction writers may have an easier time with this because if you're writing about pool designs, your potential purchasers are obviously people who sell, buy or design swimming pools.

Your website content should address a specific niche.

Again, you'll want to use "key words and phrases," that people interested in pool design will be searching on Google, Yahoo, Amazon, etc. Examples: pool design, how to build your own pool, pool services, unique pools or pool sellers.

Tip: Remember to use key words in your headlines, subheads, post descriptions and category titles. (This practice will become second nature to you as you build website pages).

· Use the best photos possible, your own if possible, especially if you are writing and discussing a topic in your field of expertise. There are also many photo sites online, both paid and free.

Dreamstime: One of the largest online photo services offering free and fee-based stock photos
Freeimages: Free and premium fee photos
Free stock photos: Over 98,000 free images available for download
Imagebase: Free photos offered by one author for a variety of public and commercial use

Fiction writers who want good content and high-quality photos will need to think more outside the box. A romance writer could focus blog posts on love stories similar to the one featured in his or her book. Or you might open a discussion on why certain types of women (like your protagonist) are attracted to certain kinds of men. Your prose style should be conversational and inviting so that your readers will feel encouraged to share their own stories or comments.

Think of it this way: direct sales pitches aren't always the most effective way to sell. Entertain your site visitors and appeal to their desires. If they can relate to your love stories or to the characters you write about, they will want to read your book.

We know ... it may seem counterintuitive but if you want to be successful, this is an approach that WORKS. Even if you pay others to do the work for you, you'll need some idea of the process to prevent getting taken to the cleaners!

Once you become more familiar with blogging and how your website promotes your online marketing, you'll be ready to implement more advanced promotional strategies.

Tip: Don't hire Uncle Angelo unless he is a true expert. Paying for quality is always a sound investment. And let's face it, it's a lot easier to fire some stranger than your mother's brother-in-law.

Advanced Website Marketing:

Author Media – web specialists sharing their knowledge with writers about successful online platform building – has outlined what readers want from author websites. Their information is based on extensive research including data from Codex Group – a "pollster for publishers."

Exclusive content is the number one reason book shoppers visit author websites according to a survey of 21,000 polled by Codex Group.

FREE is KEY. People love downloading free stories, books or coupons. We like to offer Amazon gift cards particularly during the holidays.

The best way to attract people is to set up a monthly drawing offering either a free book giveaway or an Amazon gift card. We like rafflecopter which allows you to set up and embed the giveaway on your website. Included is an option to give readers more entries to the drawing if they advertise your giveaway to their social media feeds like Facebook and Twitter.

Tip: List your giveaways with Blog Giveaway Directories for a small fee and watch your web traffic increase. Remember, once your giveaway is over, your visitor numbers may decrease but if you do this enough times and offer good content, your will slowly gain a reliable, steady following.

According to the Codex Group survey here are the other top three reasons book shoppers visit author websites:

· **Authors speaking schedule**: Of the 21,000 book buyers polled, 36 percent said they like to access speaking schedules, book signing events and author appearances.

· **Recommended Books** – at least 36 percent of shoppers surveyed said they liked reading book recommendations by authors. In addition, sample chapters or inside information on the author's own books was a plus.

Tip: If you sign up as an Amazon affiliate, you will get a small fee for any book purchased from your recommendation list.

· Book News – The Codex Group survey noted that 33 percent of those polled liked to feel they were part of the "in" crowd. They enjoy being on email alerts about future books, author events or website giveaways.

Some other marketing tips for your website:

Integrate – There are a number of tools that will connect you with new readers by sharing your content through social media links like Twitter and Facebook. Most of your website builders will offer a variety of tools. Wordpress is one of the most used site builders and every theme makes certain plugins available (i.e., site tools for sharing links, creating photo files, search engine optimization and special effects).

An easy way to promote your website or book is to pluck intriguing snippets from the articles you've written and share them on Twitter and Facebook. You can promote giveaways in the same way. Remember, the goal is reaching more people and creating interest.

#etwor k – As you continue to blog, you'll start building a team of like-minded loyalists. It's fine to ask these people if they'll mention you to their audiences and social media sites. Of course, they'll probably want a favor in return, which is actually what you're looking for.

Mutually beneficial give-and-take is a vital asset online especially if you can team up with opinion leaders. Make sure your teaming is genuine by exchanging ideas, blog posts or other information that you're excited about and always ask permission when using others'content. It's fine to take no for an answer and inquire again down the road and don't forget to follow up with non replies.

#ote: Beware of becoming an online stalker. You don't want that for yourself so respect others.

Variety of information – Use photos, videos, articles and social media sharing buttons on your website. You can reach out to other authors, book marketing experts or readers in your network list and ask them for guest posts. You can also send out tweets or Facebook requests seeking articles, photos or videos.

Recap: Build an enticing, attractive website, know your audience and go after it with quality content. Offer incentives like free gifts. Network. Don't forget to make your site marketable by using keywords in your headline, subheads and categories as well as in your post articles.

See Ad Espresso for full details and instructions
https://adespresso.com/academy/blog/5-great-ways-promote-ebook-via-facebook/

Further Reading:

Kindlepreneur - How to use and build Facebook Ads
(https://kindlepreneur.com/)

The Creative Penn – 5 ways authors can use Facebook promotions
(http://www.thecreativepenn.com/)

Twitter – A popular online community where people share thoughts and ideas. Products and news of the day as well as photos and videos have become popular posts.
#ote: Twitter posts are restricted to 140 characters.

For Beginners:

iUniverse provides instructions on how to set up your Twitter account and how to get started.
(http://www.iuniverse.com/Resources/Book-Marketing-Self-Promotion/UsingTwitterforEffectiveBookPromotion.aspx)

Your Writer Platform shows you how to get started and has more advanced instructions on how to use your account.
(http://www.yourwriterplatform.com/twitter-marketing-for-writers/)
Once you have a profile and become familiar with how to tweet, as well as how to use hashtags, mentions and retweets, you are ready to move forward.

Social Media Sun offers the following Twitter marketing tips:
(http://socialmediasun.com/how-to-promote-your-ebook-on-twitter/)

* **Use hashtags** – this helps you connect with like-minded people and potential customers.
* **Host Twitter parties** – using applications and twitter party services can help you host events such as book launches.
* **Chat rooms** – get involved in tweet chats
* **Offer** readers two or three free chapters of your book
* **Use book promotion Twitter** handles to mention your titles especially when offered for free or at a discount
* **#et work** – follow other authors, book readers, book promoters and others involved in the industry. Establish relationships so others can help you get the word out about your books, always remembering to return the favor.

#ote: When following people, you'll find that many provide a website link. Instead of reinventing the wheel, visit some of these sites to check out promotion strategies and opportunities others are offering. A book review site may want to review your book or allow you to post your profile. Another site may allow for guest posts. The possibilities are endless but you have to look for them and request permission to participate.

Go to **Social Media Sun** for detailed instructions and other links to help you with promotion ideas.
(http://socialmediasun.com/how-to-promote-your-ebook-on-twitter/)

LinkedIn – Conceived as a business forum, LinkedIn was originally a place where people posted corporate ideas, entrepreneurial events and where job seekers listed resumes. Now this business-social membership is 400 million strong and spread over 200 countries. So put on your business cap and take advantage of a huge audience.

As is customary with most online platforms, you'll need to register and create a profile. Just follow the instructions at LinkedIn. Remember to use a professional photo of yourself and a grammatically clean and interesting yet accurate description of who you are and/or what services you provide.

Since LinkedIn offers profile and group recommendations based on your information, you'll probably wish to follow or join some. The basics of engagement here are the same as other media forums: Quality content, high quality photographs, informative videos and give-and-take conversation.

Best marketing practices on LinkedIn:

#et work – Get involved with groups in your field of interest. To make it worth your time, look for groups that demonstrate active participation and list at least 20 or more participants. Be willing to help others get their messages out by sharing posts or recommendations. Usually people will return the favor without you having to ask.

Start your own Group – Build a place filled with interesting information, photos and discussions.

Paid Ads – Like Facebook, LinkedIn now allows sponsored links, information and product promotion for a fee.

Further Reading:

Business #ews Daily – 15 tips on making your name and products known
(http://www.businessnewsdaily.com/7206-linkedin-marketing-business.html)

Start a Fire – Uncommon LinkedIn marketing tips
(http://blog.startafire.com/linkedin-marketing-tips-small-businesses/)

TopRank Marketing – How to use paid sponsorship on LinkedIn (http://blog.startafire.com/linkedin-marketing-tips-small-businesses/)

#ote: It is best if you use fresh content on each site. If you don't have the time or money to hire someone, then just rewrite a paragraph or two of your original articles and make it applicable to each different audience.

Of course, you'll want to be involved with Amazon and Goodreads. These will be addressed in the next chapter.

Chapter 4:
Sell More Books on Amazon, Smashwords and Goodreads

The basics of book marketing will not change. You need to have a story or information readers want or need. Offer quality content and ensure your work is properly edited. The look of your book is as important as your prose – eye catching, searchable titles and strong book descriptions.

You will want to continue with basic online and offline book promotions by setting up book signing, author events and free or paid advertising. However, online sales – at least for self-published authors – should be your target. Build a good website, have a presence on at least one or two social media forums like Facebook, Twitter or LinkedIn, and be active on Amazon, GoodReads or Smashwords.

For writers ready for advanced marketing tools and opportunities, there are plenty to choose in the coming year. First let's take a look at how to use Amazon, GoodReads or Smashwords as these are the top 3 author platforms, at least in our opinion.

How to use Amazon to sell more books

Amazon is the world's largest online retail book store. If you list a book and leave it there, it may never sell more than a few copies but if you take the time to understand the built-in publicity tools Amazon offers, you could become a bestseller even if you never published a book before.

INDY authors should take advantage of Amazon's automated system which works to advertise all its books whether self-published or

Following is an overview of the various lists:

Recommendations Lists: Anytime you log unto Amazon or purchase a book you get a page with a number of different lists such as "recommended reads," "based on your wishlist," "kindle bestsellers," or a number of other headings. These are all compiled book titles Amazon suggests based on your search and buying habits on their site.

What this means for you as an author, is that you want your title to show up on these recommendation lists when buyers are browsing or buying books.

Here's some ideas on how to do this:

• Get more reader clicks to your book page on Amazon – this is where your other marketing comes into play. Promotions on your website, social media and paid advertising should include links directed to your Amazon book page.

Tip: At Author Marketing Club members can get instructions and book page links to direct traffic to Amazon.
(http://authormarketingclub.com/members/free-ebook-signup/)

• Run Amazon Marketing Services ads. These are available for most KDP accounts on Amazon under the "Promote and Advertise," button next to your KDP book titles. Amazon offers two types of promotions. One campaign allows your books to be promoted with other books in your genre. So when customers search "Romance," for example, Amazon will feature books in that genre based on variables in its algorithms.

A second type of promotion gives you the choice of which books you want to be promoted with by showing an impression of your title under the various "recommendation" lists every time customers buy any of the books you choose in your ad.

Authors should try to get books posted on the following list:
• Hot New Releases
• New and Noteworthy Kindle Books
• Recommended for You
• Best Seller List and Categories

Tip: If choose your book categories wisely, your book title could show up on separate category lists instead of just in one.
• Customers who bought this, also bought ...
• Amazon's Discounted Book Deals
• Kindle Unlimited Program
• Kindle Countdown Deals

Further Reading: To learn more about each of these Amazon lists and how to market your books with these promotion tools, read TCK Publishing blog written by Book Marketing Expert and Best Selling Author Tom Corson-Knowles.
(http://www.tckpublishing.com/9-amazon-book-promotion-pro-grams-that-can-help-you-sell-more-books-every-day/)

Tip: In the next chapters we also detail how to use KDP Select Free Days, .99 Deals and Kindle Unlimited marketing plans offered on Amazon.

How to use GoodReads to sell more books

A lot of authors don't use Goodreads as much as they should and it is understandable as it does take some effort to navigate through the site. But there are at least 18 million members on Goodreads, so writers should take advantage of the author tools offered free at the forum. It should be noted that Amazon acquired Goodreads in 2013 – this means that book reviews can be integrated into both sites, giving authors even more exposure.

Sometimes 100 people or more signup for the giveaways. This doesn't guarantee sales but usually a few people will buy the book if not won in the drawing.

In addition, some recommend your book to others in their friend or group circles. (Goodreads is like one big author Facebook with "likes," "recommends," "groups," and "friends.")

Book reviews often are generated from giveaways too. The more exposure your book gets, the more likely someone will buy it. Since only print giveaways are allowed, it is more likely readers will go download a digital copy if your title entices their interest.

Giveaways – The most popular author tool on Goodreads is its giveaway program. Authors are given a template allowing Goodread members to sign up for a free copy of your book. Only print books can be given for free and you are allowed to giveaway as many as you like.

Here are some tips on how to run a good giveaway as listed by Emlyn Chand at Novel Publicity:

(http://www.novelpublicity.com/2012/02/how-to-run-a-goodreads-giveaway-with-maximal-results-11-tips-we-know-youll-need/)

• Offer only 1 copy: Unless you don't mind the extra costs of shipping books to the winners, offering more than 1 copy doesn't make your campaign any more alluring.

• Autographed Books: Let readers know you will give them an autographed copy, people like these the most.

• Limit length of giveaway: Two weeks is what Goodreads

recommends. But if you limit your giveaway to 2 to 4 days, your book is likely to hit the "Newly Listed" and "Ending Soon," pages at the same time, giving you extra promotion. (The posts are similar to Amazon's varies promotion pages like "Kindle Deals," "Top 100," ect.)

• Reach out to winners: Goodreads will send you names and addresses. Prior to sending out your book contact the winner on the forum and let them know.

• Be prompt: Send prizes out right away

Read full article here: More tips in detail
(http://www.novelpublicity.com/2012/02/how-to-run-a-goodreads-giveaway-with-maximal-results-11-tips-we-know-youll-need/)

Extra Book Publicity – Here are three key tips on how to capture more book exposure during giveaways as outlined by Patrick Brown, director of marketing for Goodreads.

• **Prepublication:** people signing up for the drawing will have your title added to their "to-read" list. Once your book is published, Goodreads will send an email with the announcement to these readers.

• **Once published:** Run another giveaway. This will give you publicity with new readers or those who didn't win the prize during your prepublication may come back and give your book a second look.

Read full article: The Writer's Ally
(http://thewritersally.com/articles/how-to-use-goodreads-to-sell-more-books/)

• **Paid advertising:** With more than 300 million pageviews and 45 million unique visitors a month, this is a good investment.

• **Author profile:** Lists your bio, image and blog. You can add published works, video trailers and your recommended reads.

• **Discussion Boards:** As a member you can join groups, partake in discussion groups and list giveaways or book promotions at appropriate member sites.

Further Reading: To join Goodreads or to learn more see detailed plan here
(http://thewritersally.com/articles/how-to-use-goodreads-to-sell-more-books/)

#ote: Goodreads offers premium book advertising but it can cost up to $5,000 or more. In addition, Goodreads recommends AuthorBuzz, which has similar marketing packages but at lower costs.
(http://www.authorbuzz.com/)

How to use Smashwords to sell more books

A larger distribution is one reason over 100,000 authors around the world have published through Smashwords. Writers are not required to sign an exclusivity agreement as required through Kindle Direct Publishing at Amazon. This makes their work available to a network of retailers like Apple iBooks in 51 countries, Barnes & Noble, Kobo (which makes books available to FNAC in France and WH Smith in the U.K.), OverDrive, Gardners, Baker & Taylor and a number of library platforms.

Smashwords also allows authors to discount their books using coupons, an attractive and easy way to attract readers during title promotions. In addition, Smashwords allows preorders with a year out from publication on your book.

There are some challenges, however, to publishing on Smashwords. It is more difficult to format and upload your work on Smashwords than on Amazon and book reviews are scattered through various pages not centralized in one place like Amazon. But some authors don't want to limit their reader outreach and it is worth the extra effort to have their titles available in as many places as possible.

Marketing tools for authors at Smashwords

• **Author pages:** Similar to Amazon and Goodreads that allow you to list a profile, mug shot and information about your book. On Smashwords, however, you can list individual book pages for each work – this is similar to Fan Pages on Facebook.

• **Coupons:** This is one of the most popular features. It allows you to offer discounts or giveaways for your books. There are no stringent timelines or price requirements like Amazon.

• **Alerts:** You are allowed to embed YouTube videos promoting your book, you can upload member contributed reviews for your book and new release notifications.

• **Promotion on your Website:** Amazon does not allow you to have excerpts or sell your KDP Select books directly from you website. With Smashword widgets and coupons you can sell direct from your website too.

For further reading: Smashwords – Details as well as free setup and marketing guides available here
(https://www.smashwords.com/about/supportfaq)

Sell more Books in 2017 using #ew Internet Tools

As technology continues to take over our everyday tasks, people are turning more toward mobile applications and quick downloads on their tablets. Authors need to be where their customers shop so along with all the other necessary skills required for the savvy writer, digital advertising should be on the learning list.

Pinterest – This site has become very popular online. It is a combination of a digital pin-up board and a scrapbook. It's like Twitter only instead of 140-character messages, you use pictures and videos.

(https://www.pinterest.com/)

Great content, good photos and author engagement are essential. No different than any other electronic forum but this site relies more on visuals than any other platform. Beth Hayden, a social media expert and author of Pinfluence:

(https://www.amazon.com/Pinfluence-Complete-Marketing-Business-Pinterest/dp/1118393775)

The Complete Guide to Marketing your Business with Pinterest, advises the following 7 tips:

- Create an Author Board: This is your profile. Make it interesting.
- Post pictures of readers with your Book
- Dedicate a board for each of your titles
- Link to all your blogs, events and promotions
- Pin images and videos of book signing or author events
- Create a Board for your book recommendations
- Be a trusted curator: You can post articles about your niche or other author information

Further Reading: To learn more about these book marketing ideas as well as other promotional concepts see bookbaby Blog

(http://blog.bookbaby.com/2012/07/7-ways-to-sell-more-books-with-pinterest/)

Snapchat - is one of the hottest mobile messaging applications on the market. It allows you to add captions and text to your photos and videos and is a fun way to keep connected with family and friends without using up all your phone's memory.

Millennials use snapchat most making this application popular with a lot of college students. Research also shows user like using coupons and discount codes to make purchases online from their phones, according to a report by Writers Weekly.

(http://writersweekly.com/article-use-snapchat)

Authors should tap into this by offering free books, discounted webinars or coupons toward their products. Also make yourself interesting by posting good content and interesting photos. Like other social mediums snapchat is a mini-forum where you have a few seconds to grab your readers and keep them interested enough to come back or to buy your products.

Further Reading:
Giving Books a Voice – Offers data and statistics on why authors need to use snapchat to sell books.

(http://givingbooksavoice.com/cgi-sys/suspendedpage.cgi)

Mashable - Beginners Guide to Snapchat
(http://mashable.com/2014/08/04/snapchat-for-beginners/#1ImvBAUovZq3)

Tom Blubaugh, a literary strategist, has an article titled, Authors: Can Snapchat help you Sell Books, offers some ideas on how to engage with your audience and what type of fun photos to post. We recommend reading the full article.

(http://tomblubaugh.net/writing/authors-can-snapchat-help-you-sell-books.html)

In addition, more online retailers are distributing ebooks and offering a variety of platforms for new titles to be discovered. You should at least become familiar with these opportunities and when able use them to your advantage. One way to do so is with preorders.

Preorders – Smashwords and Amazon (Kindle Direct Publishing) – two top e-book retailers – allow customers to buy books ahead of its release. An option offered for free to authors registered at these sites. Yet, many writers don't use this tool in spite of evidence that preorders sell more copies overall.

Before launching your preorder campaign, you should become familiar with the guidelines at Smashwords and Amazon.

• **Release Date** – Decide when you want your titles to be made available for preorder purchases. Some authors prefer a short pre-launch promotion, where others see long-term publicity to be more beneficial.

a. Amazon allows preorders up to 90 days before your book is released.

b. Smashwords has teamed with Assetless which offer a 12 preorder, with distribution to iBooks, Barnes & Noble and Kobo.

• Pricing – Research shows that buyers purchase more ebooks when titles cost between .99 and $4.99.

• **How to promote** –

• Talk about it on your website. Ask your readers to help you get the word out or offer some type of contest giving the person that offers the most tweets for you on Twitter a free copy of the book and maybe a Starbucks coffee coupon.

• Set up a Twitter campaign

• Mention your preorders on your Fan pages on Facebook. You may want to create a new Fan page just for your preorder too.

• Look for blogs you can guest post on about your new book

• Post a video – like a book trailer or infomercial – on your website, social media forums and on Youtube.

Further Reading:

Author Marketing Experts – This article shows authors how to use and set up preorders on Amazon.

(https://www.amarketingexpert.com/boost-book-amazons-pre-order/)

Mark Coker, Smashwords Founder, offers his expertise on a guest post at PublishersWeekly.

(http://www.publishersweekly.com/pw/by-topic/authors/pw-select/article/68748-how-indie-authors-can-use-preorders-to-crack-the-bestseller-lists.html)

Chapter 5: How to Use Free Book Promotions on Amazon and Smashwords

Most authors publish their books through Amazon via Createspace or Smashwords. Both programs offer digital publishing and electronic distribution. Both sites also allow authors to pitch their work for free – a publicity practice that was popular when digital publishing took off on Amazon. While Smashwords allows no cost listing at the author's discretion, Amazon allows up to five days free within a 90 day window. If you enroll in the Amazon Kindle Direct Publishing program, there is an inclusivity clause forcing authors to publish and distribute only through Amazon.

Here's an overview:

Smashwords – "To many authors, the idea of giving their work away for free is counterintuitive—and possibly abhorrent and sacrilegious. Free devalues your work, right?"

Mark Coker, Smashwords founder says "No."

Visibility is the biggest reason to offer your work free. It's a win-win for both reader and author. Writers reach an audience who wouldn't normally take a chance on an unknown author and readers have no financial risk.

"Free e-books get 41 times more downloads on average than other e-books," according to a 2015 Smashwords Survey. "Free drives sampling and discovery."

To read Mark Coker's full article on this subject, click here: (https://www.smashwords.com/books/view/305)

Smashword FREE offers:

Before you upload your final product for publication on Smashwords and its various distribution centers, make sure you have top quality:

• Book Cover

• Clean content

• Great Title (when possible using "searchable" keywords and if you can't use the keywords in your headline, then use subheads)

• Great book description

• FREE price

Tip: Since Smashwords uses coupons to offer discounts on your books, you don't have to initially list your book for free as you can offer the discount coupons at a later date.

Promoting: Marketing efforts are conducted through your blogs and social media sites. In addition, Smashwords offers a free marketing guide.

Most of the online forums are dedicated to promoting Kindle Books but there are some sites available for Nook and Kobo titles, which are also part of your Smashwords distribution.

Here are #ook and Kobo sites:

Kobo Book Hub

Nook and Kobo

Nook Boards

Nook Lovers

Story Finds

Most of the Free Kindle Promotion sites will also accept your Free Promotions on Smashwords. However, because readers and book submission marketers don't like to deal with the Smashword coupons, some forums won't accept Smashword titles.

CHECK SITE RULES BEFORE
UPLOADI#G YOUR BOOK

Here is a link to 90 Free Book Promotion sites:
(https://jamescalbraith.com/2013/01/09/80-sites-to-advertise-your-book/)

The following platforms offer paid publicity for all digital books:

Booktastik – (One of the newer advertising sites specializing in cheap book promotions, including Kindle, Nook, B&N, etc. If your book is either free, or discounted, chances are they'll advertise it for you. Their prices are very reasonable – between $5 and $10 depending on the genre that your book is in.)

Ebook Soda – (One of the newer players in the book promotion game, Ebook Soda still boasts a very respectable 14,000 email subscriber list, as well as over 8,000 Facebook page likes.

As befits a smaller kindle promotions group, their pricing is straight forward: $15 to promote your Amazon Kindle or Nook novel and an additional $6 if you want your book to be shared on the EbookSoda Twitter page.)

Ereaders #ews – This site has a Facebook page of more than 500,000 fans. Though their ebook promotion pricing is very competitive (between $25 and $110 depending on your promotion) they do have a list of Promotion Requirements they strictly adhere to that precludes erotica as well as the requirement that your book is over 125 pages (exceptions: Children's Stories or

Cook Books.) They advertise on Amazon Kindle as well as on Barnes and Noble – Nook, Apple iBooks, Google Play, Kobo and Sony Reader. They also have a dedicated Christian Fiction Promotion section, so if your book falls into that category, ENT is likely to be one of the best promotions groups for your ebook.)

KDP Select - After you have written a quality book and have it professionally edited, follow the next steps and publish on Kindle Direct Publishing Select. You can either use Createspace or upload the book yourself at: Amazon.

a. Choose a good cover, title and seven solid keywords

b. Determine your 2 categories and narrow your choices to tight, focused subcategories

c. Write a great book description

d. List your book on Kindle Direct Publishing Select

Since Amazon changed the rules in March 2012, KDP Select is no longer a sure thing. But FREE Days can still generate book sales and in our opinion, in spite of the exclusivity rules on Amazon, KDP Select is the best route for first time authors. Before you start:

At setup -
1. Choose effective keywords
2. Pick two categories
3. Write a spot-on book description
4. Select your promotion dates for listing your book free
5. Announce your free day dates 14 to 30 days ahead of time at all relevant promotion sites
6. Be ready for promo days

Your action Plan:

There are several sites that will post your KDP Promotions for FREE. Others require payment for a guaranteed placing, including our site, Kindle Book Promos. This is due to a change in the way Amazon promotes free books and how it pays its affiliates – people like us that promote Amazon books.

Are you ready to promote? Make sure your book is properly listed, formatted, titled and has an interesting and appropriate cover. Be prepared to list your book at numerous sites on promotion days, be willing to respond to emails and blog requests and follow up your free days with additional marketing.

Advertise Free Days: The more sites and forums that hear about your book, the more successful your campaign will be. Get the news out to every social site you frequent and post to every network open to book promotions.

These three sites offer a list of Free Promotion Listings and submission tools for FREE:

FREE Kindle Book Submission Tool

http://authormarketingclub.com/members/submit-your-book/

Over 120 sites to promote your FREE DAYS

http://www.creativindie.com/turbo-charge-your-ebook-promotion-with-110/

For all your different Kindle Book Promotions

http://www.ebookbooster.com/

**Here are some of the top sites we use to promote our
KDP-Select Free Days:**

#ote : (You can Google the sties or send me an email at kindlebookpromos@gmail.com and I will send you the PDF of our Kindle Version which includes all the links.)

Addicted to eBooks
Ask David
Author Marketing Club
Awesome Gang
Bargain Booksy
Bargain eBook Hunter
Book Barbarian – SciFi and Fantasy
Book Bear
Book Bongo
BookBub
Book Goodies
Book Gorilla
Book of the Day
BookSliced
BookStar
Book Swag
Booktastik
Digital Book Today
Daily Cheap Reads
Ebooksforfreeinc
eBook Lister

eBook Soda
eBook Stage
Ereader News Today
Flurries Unlimited
Free Book Dude
Free Booksy
Free eBooks Daily
Free Kindle Books and Tips
Frugal Freebies
Good Kindles
InkArcade
Indie Book Lounge
Indies Unlimited
justkindlebooks
Kindle Boards
Kindle Book Promos
Kindle Book Review
Kindle Nation Daily
Masquerade Crew
My Book Cave
PeopleReads
Pixel Scroll
Planet eBooks (US & UK)
Read Freely
Reading Deals
Ripley's Booklist – Young Adult Books
Steamy Romance Stories (Romance)
The Books Machine
The Choosy Bookworm
The Digital Ink Spot
The Ereader Cafe

The Fussy Librarian
World Literary Cafe

Here are sites we recommend for paid advertising of your FREE DAYS:
(Remember there are no guarantees for book sales.)

Kindle Book Promos –
(Our site offers very reasonable prices)
http://kindlebookpromos.luckycinda.com

BookBub - (Your book has to be accepted first)

Book Butterfly – (Different promotional packages)

Book Gorilla - (Fairly new site)

Book Kitty – (The price is right – $5)

Book Sends -
(Fairly new site but run by a savvy author/marketer)

Book Tweeting Service-
(A bit pricey but good service with a large audience)

Digital Book Today-
(Great site, good promotion opportunities and run by a
book-savvy author and all-around great guy)

Ereaders #ews – (This site has a Facebook page of more than
500,000 fans. Though their ebook promotion pricing is very competitive,
being between $25 and $110 depending on your promotion, they do have a

list of Promotion Requirements that they adhere to strictly, which precludes erotica, as well as the requirement that your book is over 125 pages (except for Children's Stories or Cook Books.)

Free Kindle Books and Tips – (The self-proclaimed "Home of the #1 subscription Amazon Kindle blog." If you choose to advertise, your book's details will go out to over 675,000 Kindle readers, including: Over 600,000 people accessing the blog via the free reader app or the Collections app for their Kindle Fire, and more than 150,000 people via an e-Ink Kindle subscription, email or social media subscription, or directly on the blog's website, or via an RSS reader.)

> Just Kindle Books –
> (promotional options starting at $15, and going up to a modest $35)

> Kindle Boards – (Slots fill up fast so make sure to coordinate your promo days accordingly.)

> The Kindle Book Review - (Operated by a best-selling author and his team who are very helpful to authors.)

> One Hundred Free Books – (Their prices start at $75 and increase to $100 for "prominent placement in all comunications", which includes not only their Facebook page, but also their email subscription list.)

> Your Book Promoter – (Good site with Twitter, Facebook and online book promotions between $49 and $249.)
> Use Twitter and Facebook on the Day of your Promotions:

#o te: Be careful not to spam – spread your tweets throughout the promotion dates. Don't blast every 10 minutes to each site. You should post to Facebook sites only once per day unless you have permission by the site administrator to do otherwise. And since Facebook has very strict rules about free advertising, don't get kicked off.

#ote: Self-Publishing Review offers an inside look at how to use twitter services with data, templates, results and a list of sites to post your message.

When using Twitter, you will want to use hashtags with keywords and when possible use images.

Use the following hashtags and keywords on Twitter to promote your free days:

#kindle
#kindlefire
#ebooks
#FREE
#mustread
#goodreads
#greatreads
#freeebooks
#Kindlefreebooks
#AmazonPrime
#Kindledeals
#kindledeals

Example: Winner of 5 literary awards, #FREE today on #kindle: (your link here)

You can also hashtag genre references, like #romance, #mystery, #nonfiction – whatever applies to your title. Or hashtag your audience, for example if your book has an educational target:

#teachers, #education or #learningtools.

Also let these Twitter sites know about your free books and ask for a retweet or mention. For example if you wanted us to retweet your free book day, you would contact us either @freebookpromos or @penabook.

This is how:

@freebookpromos Pls RT: #FREE today (your title or genre) on #kindle: (your link)

(Remember you only have 140 characters total – so keep it short).

Here are other sites: (There are many so don't limit your promotion to these – you can search for more on Twitter using the search box or add to your list as you come across sites in books or other blogs you use):

@bookbub
@Booksontheknob
@Bookyrnextread
@CheapKindleDly
@DigitalBkToday
@digitalinktoday
@fkbt
@free
@freebookclub1
@freebookdude
@Freebookdeal
@freebookpromos
@freeebooksdaily
@freebooksy
@freedailybooks
@4FreeKindleBook
@free_kindle
@FreeKindleStuff
@FreeReadFeed
@free2kindle

@IndAuthorSucess
@IndieKindle
@ibdbookoftheday
@KindleBookBlast
@KindleBookKing
@Kindlbookreview
@KindleDaily
@KindleEbooksUK
@kindlenews
@kindle_free
@Kindlefreebies
@KindleFreeBook
@kindlefreebooks
@kindle_mojo
@Kindle_promo
@kindlestuff
@KindleUpdates
@penabook
@pixelofink
@WLCPromotions
@zilchebooks

Facebook sites that allow free book day postings:
Amazon Kindle
Bargain Ebook Hunter
Book Club Girl
Book Goodies
Book Lovers Haven
Book Riot
Canada Kindle Books
Digital Book Today
Ebook Promos

Book Club Girl
Book Goodies
Book Lovers Haven
Book Riot
Canada Kindle Books
Digital Book Today
Ebook Promos
Ebooks FreeFreeFree
Free Book Club
Free Book Feed
Free Book Today
Free Books
Free Kindle Books
Free Today on Amazon
FreeBooksy - (Has a list of other Free Book Listing Sites)
Galley Cats
iAuthor
Indie Book Lounge
Indie Books List
Kindle Bestseller List
Kindle Obsessed
Mobile Read
New Free Kindle Books
One Hundred Free Books
Promote kdBook Free
Story Finds
The Kindle Book Review
UK Book Lovers
We Love Books
World Literary Cafe

Chapter 6:
Kindle Countdown Promos and
$.99 Kindle Deals

Not that long ago, Amazon treated "free promotion" downloads like "book sales." This meant that an unknown author could become a bestseller without generating any sales income. Here's how it worked: In Amazon advertising, the most-downloaded titles appeared next to traditionally published bestsellers, making it seem like the free books had achieved bestseller status. And even when Amazon allowed you to up the price after a free promotion date, your book would continue to sell and get downloaded because it stayed on the ranking list for at least a week.

In 2014, when giveaway promotions started to fade due to a rewrite of Amazon rules, the $.99 Kindle Deal replaced "free," a change that came about due to pressure exerted by the Big 5 publishers. A giveaway no longer counted as a sale and the top free downloads no longer sat next to bestsellers; you'd have to click on a link to see the bestselling free books.

That is where $.99 promotions came in.

When this marketing tool first became available, it took off. Recently, however, its popularity has waned a bit but the $.99 options can still help work by new authors be discovered.

A second price-related publicity strategy is called Kindle Countdown promos, which allows authors to pitch their books for up to two weeks at different prices. For example, you can offer your book for $.99 for three days, then mark up the price to $1.99 for a few days and then up it again to $2.99 for the remainder of your campaign. This is a great tool for finding new readers while experimenting with different price points.

The following information details the ins and outs of $.99 deals and countdown promos on Amazon and can be applied to your work on Smashwords.

#ote: Remember, you must be exclusive to Amazon to take advantage of its various Kindle platforms so you won't be able to publish the same titles on KDP Select and Smashwords at the same time.

Let's take a look at how $.99
and Countdown Promos can help you.

Advantages:

* Most buyers are willing to risk $.99 for a book even if they don't know the author.

* If you have more than one title, the $.99 book could draw readers to your other work.

* There are many sites that welcome $.99 titles so they're easier to pitch than higher priced books.

* You could increase book sales.

* Since digital books don't cost you printing or shipping costs, every sale is profit.

Disadvantages:

* You don't make as much because Amazon only pays 35 percent royalty on books priced under $2.99. Books priced $2.99 or higher receive 70 percent royalty. This means you'd need to sell more books at 99 cents than you would books priced at $2.99 or higher to make the same revenue.
* Your book may have a lower perceived value by readers.

How to promote $.99 cent deals:

Some authors have made their books permanently free. Instead of sales, these writers are seeking to brand themselves and build a following for future work. The same approach could be applied to a 99 cent title: Instead of making zero profit, you could take in some revenue while positioning yourself. We sold our ebook marketing title, Sell more Ebooks – how to increase sales and Amazon rankings using Kindle Direct Publishing at $.99 for several months, landing us on several top 20 category lists. In addition, we earned many positive reviews and increased our following at Kindle Book Promos – a site dedicated to the promotion of authors and their books.

Before you start: The basics still apply: You need a professional cover, great book description and some positive book reviews. Since reviews are an important part of your overall book package, I've included a brief overview of their how-tos.

Why reviews are important:

Book reviews matter; they're the street cred builders for new authors and new releases. Amazon uses book reviews and customer satisfaction ratings as part of their ranking formula for all their Top 100 lists. Customers rely on reviews to determine whether they want to buy an item and publishers seeking new talent also keep an eye on these statistics.

How to get reviews:

a. At the end of your published work, ask for a book review and provide a link for the reader.

b. If you have the $400 per review from reputable critics like Kirkus or Publisher Weekly, take advantage. Note: Most readers today don't put a lot of stock in high-profile reviews because they're more interested in what their friends and neighbors think. However, book stores, traditional publishers and libraries still value big-name reviews for their evaluations ... so if you're targeting these places and have the money, go for it.

c. Include book review requests at the end of blog posts within author-friendly forums, in your tweets or as part of your social media posts.

d. Contact Review Bloggers – Search for book review sites using keywords associated with your story. Or, just type, "Book Review Blogs." All potential reviewers have their own unique requirements – some may wish to be queried first while some prefer hard cover copies to digital files.

Paid vs Free reviews:

A number of new book review services have appeared in response to the ever growing crush of self-publishers looking for quotable evaluations. But you have to be careful. While there are professionals and reputed critics offering reviews for a fee, others are only interested in taking your money.

Fake reviews and other marketing ploys forced Amazon to create new policies. This caused a great deal of confusion as not all were well publicized. For unspecified reasons, many book reviews disappeared overnight. Some sites were forced to shut down and some authors were actually removed from Amazon's site. Now that the dust has settled, things seem to be running more smoothly.

Clarification: On Amazon, you can gift your book for a review but the reviewer should disclose that fact when posting an evaluation. In addition:

"Paid reviews are welcome in the 'Editorial Reviews' section of a book's detail page. Reviews written for any form of compensation other than a free copy of the product are not allowed in the Customer Reviews section."

To pay or not to pay ... up to you. A respectable rave could help you with advertising but paid or not, even a fantastic review doesn't guarantee sales.

Once your book is ready, start your promotion. There are numerous sites that for small fees will post $.99 promotions through newsletters or site subscriptions. SEO efforts (making your book searchable through the blogging you do on social media and your website) will also help customers find your work.

Listing your 99 cent promos – the following sites have high-ranking Alexa, meaning you have the potential to reach a higher number of readers when you list or advertise on these blogs.

Awesome Gang

Bargain Booksy –
Not as pricey as Bookbub but more costly than other sites.
Still, a nice platform for promoting.

Bargain eBook Hunter
Bibliotastic
Book Daily
Book Deal Hunter
Book Goodies
Bookbear

BookBub – on the pricey side – and you must be pre-approved. But if you have the right type of book, big sales are possible.

Books Butterfly
Buck Books

Daily Free ebooks – Don't let the site name fool you! This forum is no longer a free ebook promotion service; it's dedicated to books costing 99 cents or less.

Ebook Stage
Ereader News Today
Fire and Ice Book Tours
Free Discounted Books
Get Free Ebooks
GoodKindles
Just Kindle Books
Kindle Book Promos – free and paid promotions available.
Kindle Nation Daily
Kufads
Many Books
Obooko
Read Cheaply
Spoiled Reader
Steamy Romance Books
StoryFinds
The Fussy Librarian
The Independent Author Network
The Kindle Book Review

The Wall of Books
The Women's Nest
Zwoodle Books

The following three sites are also high-ranking Alexa blogs but you have to be a member or pay for advertising to take advantage of the premium features available. We have used all three in the past with success. In addition we are members and affiliates of The Author Marketing Club.

The Author Marketing Club – Membership is required access all the great marketing tools, such as book description formatting software for Kindle, which creates an appealing list of your books and converts it to a widget for your blog. This forum also offers free marketing videos and many other helpful applications. The cost is around $100 for one year or you can pay month to month which adds up to a higher annual fee.

#ote: A basic membership is free. You don't have access to all the cool tools but you'll still qualify for some great benefits: A forum to list your books for reviews, a tool to submit your free days to several promotion sites and access to many affordable advertising opportunities. We recommend this site.

World Literary Cafe – This is a great site so if you haven't joined, do so. You'll find opportunities to increase your Twitter and Facebook followings. In addition, the Cafe has twitter teams to help get your tweets to a larger audience – especially helpful when running promotions. The site also features book reviews, blog requests and book marketing forums. Finally, the site hosts 99 cent Fridays and a slew of other marketing opportunities, including some free options.

Book Tweeting Service – This site has a large audience of active book buyers. On one occasion, we used the service for two days and sold 63 books. During another promotion, we used the service for two days and only sold 12 books. Even so, the service is good and the followers are legit people looking for books.

Good Twitter Sites:
https://twitter.com/ebooks99cents
https://twitter.com/99KindlePromos
https://twitter.com/99ebooks
https://twitter.com/KindleSwag
https://twitter.com/CrazyKindle
https://twitter.com/99centsale
https://twitter.com/book_tribe
https://twitter.com/AllKindleDeals

#ow let's take a look at Kindle Countdown Book Promotions:
This tool allows authors to advertise limited-time discounts on their ebooks. Your countdown deal can last up to two weeks and is a "hyper-focused" type of sale. Via this program, you can continue to earn your selected royalty rate during the promotion. So instead of the 35 cents per ebook you'd receive when priced at $.99 cents (due to Amazon's 35 percent royalty for titles priced under $2.99), each sale would generate 70 cents during the countdown deal.

Amazon is still experimenting with Countdown Deals and hasn't advertised them as well as KDP – Select promotions. We've come across authors who are unenthusiastic about Countdown Deals but, like most marketing plans, if executed properly, this tool can help generate more sales.

Advantages:

* You set the dates and the discount price, which means you can plan your marketing efforts in advance. Like the Free Day promos, sites are available to advertise your deals, including a couple that can lead to a significant number of downloads.

* Amazon has its own dedicated website for readers, making your titles more visible.

* Kindle Countdown offers a totally cool price raise" feature that allows authors and publishers to set the discounted price as low as $.99 cents, then incrementally raise it to full price as the days go on. Amazon even posts a countdown clock next to your title alerting customers how long they have left until the sale ends.

Criteria:

1) Your book has to be enrolled in KDP Select for at least 30 days before a Kindle Countdown Deal can be triggered.

2) You cannot run a KDP Select free promotion and a Kindle Countdown Deal in the same 90-day period.

3) The program is only open to US and UK markets.

After you set up your Kindle Countdown Deal at Amazon, you will want to market the promotion like any other campaign – use free and paid advertisement, post on your social media sites and contact your customer list.

Places to post your Kindle Countdown deals:
Book Goodies
Books Machine
Digital Ink Today
Digital Book Today - selling a variety of author services.
E-Reader News
Kindle Book Promos – offering free and paid listings

World Literary Cafe -
running $.99 Fridays. It costs $20 to participate.

Further Reading: Author Rachael K. Burke has a long list of places to promote your Countdown Deal, give it a read and help her out by buying a few of her books. Let her know we sent you!
(http://www.rachelkburke.com/2017/01/best-websites-for-your-kindle-countdown.html)

Good FACEBOOK sites to list your promos:
Ebookpromos – List your Countdown Deals here.
KindleCountdownDeals –
Open group, make sure to follow forum rules.

Kindle Countdown and $.99 Deals
Ereader News Today – Lists bargain books.

Twitter:
@EbookCountdown
@KindleDailyDeal
@kindledeals
@freebookpromos
@CrazyKindle
@AllKindleDeals
@KindleDeals_
@ShopKindleDeals

Chapter 7:
Get your Books
into Stores and Libraries

The most common question we hear from Indie writers is: How do you get your titles onto the shelves of book retailers and libraries? As this is a totally separate endeavor, you'll need a budget for offline marketing.

#OTE: Marketing hard copy books is every bit as challenging as pitching titles online and, in some instances, will take more time and money. That's why you need a BUSINESS PLAN comprised of REALISTIC expenses PRIOR to publishing.

First, let's explore how book stores interact with self-published novels.

How can I sell to Bookstores?

Costs, quality, distribution and inventory are all considerations when book stores consider acquisitions. This is why working with established people in the business is easier but there are some book buyers willing to take a chance on self-published creators who operate like traditional sellers.

* Costs:

a. Bookstores prefer ordering through major suppliers because it reduces paperwork. Money is saved when a few invoices versus thousands are processed.

b. Print-On-Demand is more expensive than offset printing.

c. Major book suppliers offer 35 to 55 percent discounts to book stores whereas self-publishing suppliers, like Createspace (through Amazon), only offer 25 percent or less.

d. Self-Published writers often overprice their books making it more difficult for sales with other similar titles marked down.

#ote: When dealing with independent or smaller book stores than the larger retailers like Barnes & Nobles, placing titles on consignment is more common. Also some of the discount and pricing can be negotiated because you will be dealing one-on-one in most cases. The same rules still apply: Costs, quality, distribution and inventory.

* **Quality:** What is the look of your book? First impressions matter to consumers, even more so on a shelf with numerous other books.

Following are some suggestions for good cover designs excerpted from our book, *Sell more Ebooks – How to increase sales and Amazon rankings using Kindle Direct Publishing*:

Invoke an emotional response with eye-grabbing ideas

a. Believe it or not, less IS more.

Keep it clean and leave plenty of "white space" (empty area). Try to avoid too much fancy artwork or complicated designs that detract from the title or main thrust of the cover art and make sure your fonts can be easily read!aWhat type of covers pique your interest? Look at books in your genre – and in your personal library – to see what styles or layouts appeal to you most.

b. Mood Indigo - Setting the stage:

The colors and images you use should evoke feelings/impressions in potential buyers. Determine what type of reaction you are seeking and do some research on how to produce that reaction visually.

USA Today took some jabs from design dilettantes and journalism traditionalists on the launch of its newspaper in 1982. Today the Gannet-owned publication is one of the most widely circulated newspapers in the United States.

c. Is a picture worth 1,000 words? Artwork is crucial.

Your cover is the potential buyer's first introduction to your labor of love and its content.

d. You need a backbone! Don't forget the spine.

For those of you that desire both digital and print copies, it's important to remember that when standing upright on a shelf, the spine may be all that's visible to a potential reader. This makes it valuable space. The spine should display your name and book title.

#ote:

Inside Layout - Make sure your inside pages are as professional as your cover design. You don't want hanging words, misplaced sentences or blurry images.

Back Cover – The back of your book should be as enticing as the front. A great book description, a professional mug of yourself and a barcode with price and genre of your title.

Price – Finally, your book needs to be priced in the $15 to $20 range to compete with other books

Content:

Professional Editing: If you want to secure buyers and keep them coming back for more, make sure their experience with your manuscript is a pristine one. Present error-free copy with professional quality content and copy editing, design and formatting.

Accidental grammar errors, misplaced punctuation, and unintentionally misspelled words will all bounce a reader right out of the text, no matter how poetic or life-altering. The money you spend on professional help – an editor, a copy editor and a proof reader – is the soundest investment you can make in your product.

Distribution and Inventory:

Bookstores don't want to be stuck with your book. Buy backs is one reason these retailers prefer dealing with traditional publishers. Bookstores need the assurance that publishers will buy back unsold books – not always the case with P.O.D. copies. You could offer to buy back the P.O.D. leftovers yourself but it will cost you more than it did to print the book.

Some authors like to use short print runs rather than printing on demand. This means that bulk printing – like 200 or more books at a time – is produced instead of printing a title only when it is bought (P.O.D.).

#ot e: Most distributors want to work with publishers that have a catalog of books instead of representing individual titles. There's also fees to consider. Distributors want a percentage of royalties for books sold, some charge storage and shipping fees and don't forget that your book will be discounted up to 55 percent when sold to sellers.

This is where P.O.D. services like Lightning Source and IngramSpark will be a better choice. These services allow book buy backs and as distributors Ingram is very respected and known in the business.

Further Reading: Self-Publishing review offers a list of distributors as well as other tips on selling to book stores and places to purchase marketing packages. BookLife by Publisher's Weekly also has an article with an inside look at selling to bookstores a n d libraries.

So how do you find bookstores and who do you contact?

Public libraries and phone books are the best resources to find business listings. But there's nothing like engine searches online. You can google, bing or yahoo "local bookstores," "independent book shops," or a number of other terms related to what you are seeking.

Here's some sites to get you started:

American Bookseller Association – Click under membership and go to the directory. This will let you search for stores by name or city. There are numerous other author tools available on this site.

Barnes & #obles – There is also a link on the site for authors and publishers detailing submission queries to sell in its stores.

Books a Million – Click store locator at top of page.

When looking for stores in your area decide how far you are willing to drive. Keep in mind that you need to budget for gasoline and lodging. Also the further away you get from home, the less likely radio and newspapers will promote you for free unless you have some type of local tie-in for their area, so budget for additional advertising in the media.

Book signing tips:
Talk to store managers before dropping in. Bigger shops will have a book buyer or acquisition specialist. Before you call do your research, make sure your type of genre is sold at the location. Also have a marketing plan on how you will get people to the bookstore for an author signing or book event.

Managers will love free publicity in newspapers, radio or online advertising. If they get more customer traffic then they will be more willing to work with an unknown writer.

If there is no interest, ask if you can call back in a few weeks. Or drop by in a few weeks and tell them you were in the neighborhood and wanted to follow up on your previous call. If you are turned down always ask why, maybe there is something you can fix for a future yes.

When given the thumbs up, find out what works for book signings. How many books should you bring, what type of discounts are you willing to offer and can you leave any autographed copies behind to sell after the event.

#ote: At mom and pop shops you will usually leave books on consignment or the store owner will buy a handful of copies outright. Make sure you have any deal you make in writing. Remember autographed copies are popular.

Now let's take a look at getting books into libraries.

How to Sell to Libraries

Getting hard copy books into libraries is difficult for any author not just new writers. But the lower cost of ebooks for cash-strapped bibliotheca is attractive and a door has been open for self-published authors. With more than 16,000 public libraries, plus thousands of university and other types of athenaeums.

These institutions frown on self-produced products for the same reasons as bookstores: Costs, quality, distribution and inventory. Libraries also rely on book reviews by Library Journal or Kirkus Reviews.

#ote: Midwest Book Review is also reputable and it is open to quality self-produced products.

Costs:

Libraries don't have a lot of revenue so acquisition specialists are selective with book buys. Additionally, libraries base purchases according to the "collection development policy" that governs its facilities. This policy calls for a title to have been reviewed in an established periodical. Here's a preferred list of survey publications: Referenced under Reviews (scroll toward bottom of page).

#ote: Local bibliothecas are allowed to buy some books from local writers under their guidelines but that doesn't mean your book will be bought at other libraries. Keep in mind that libraries buy books using a purchase order number and then pay the invoice at a later date.

Quality:

If your book is professional, it should look no different than any other "bestseller" from the Big 5 publishers: Eye-catching title, cover, and back cover designed with book description, author bio, price and genre.

We suggest you visit the library first and scan the shelves for the genre you are pitching. For example, some libraries may be overstocked on World War II titles or How-To books for certain topics. The higher demand for your content, the higher chance for more sales. Fiction books are also more popular than non-fiction. Speak with the librarian or the person in charge of buying books.

Sturdy books printed on acid-free (alkaline) paper are desirable. Remember your book has the potential to be borrowed a few times, you don't want to have a product that falls apart when a reader handles it. In addition, the type of print used is important because pages printed on acid paper become too brittle after 50 years or more.

Distribution:
Baker & Taylor and Ingram Library Services are two of the most widely used suppliers for public, academic and technical information centers. Buying directly from publishers is also common. For independent writers, traditional distribution is not cost efficient, especially if only a handful of books get sold. The good news is the digital world has continued to evolve and with it so has acceptance for all types of authors. Libraries too are going digital and have turned to electronic catalogues provided through various venues – OverDrive on Smashwords, one of the most used.

Further Reading: You should become familiar with Library of Control numbers and other coding that librarians use to locate books for purchase. Instead of going into lengthy details and adding more confusion to the already surmountable information necessary to make it in this business, go to The Book Designer.

Before proceeding, let's take a brief look at digital distribution options:

NEWEST Program: Library Journal and BiblioBoard – an ebook publisher – has teamed to aid non-traditional publishers into the library market. A program known as SELF-e allows authors into the complex world of the library market. The catch – you make no royalties.

But it gives you a chance to place your book in front of the information centers at your state and national level that previously were not allowed. It also gets your work vetted by Library Journal, the national publication and most relied on by libraries when making book purchase decisions.

BiblioBoard is used to display your ebooks to more than 2,700 libraries and reaches some 30 million patrons.

Read more about the program here: Self-e Library Journal.

In addition, authors can now get into libraries and make small profits through ebooksareforever and Overdrive on Smashwords.

Once your book is ready to be sold, the best method of making library sales is direct queries. When writing be sure to include all necessary information about your book and yourself. If you have an idea for a book event or writing class, include the plans in your letter.

Further Reading: To get you started, here is an article by Romance University offering advice from a librarian who buys books. Also included on the site is an example query letter to send. At Writer's Beware, another librarians offers the "do" and "don't" tips of selling books to libraries.

Other methods of becoming visible:

* Advertising - with American Library Association's well-known media forums

* Direct Mail/Library Lists – If you send books to libraries without its request your book may end up in the donation pile that later gets sold at fundraisers. So don't just send a book hoping for the best.

* Authors for Libraries - Connecting Authors & Libraries – This program offers a list of resources about author visits and partnership opportunities between writers and library groups.

Further Reading:
For a list of links and detailed practices on all these points:
(http://www.ala.org/tools/libfactsheets/alalibraryfactsheet05)

American Library Association:
A list of article on how to market to libraries

The Combined Book Exhibit: Marketing to Libraries

Lucinda Sue Crosby and Laura Dobbins

Final Thoughts

Dear Readers:

As you can see marketing is a full-time job and it can be daunting. Most writers would rather spend time producing plots then trying to sell them. Personally, we would so much rather produce ingenious plots or fascinating characters than tackle sales but alas, in today's very competitive publishing environment, self-promotion is an absolute necessity.

We hope we have given you some tools and advise to get you started. Pick one or two and if it works for you, stick with that. Don't try to tackle everything at once, it will be too overwhelming.

We appreciate your time and we wish you much success. Should you have any questions, please don't hesitate to email:

kindlefreebies@yahoo.com. Please see our book site for a number of author and book promotion and features: Kindle Book Promos.

http://kindlebookpromos.luckycinda.com

Thanks! Laura and Lucinda Sue

PS: If you enjoyed this book please leave us a review on Amazon.

Lucinda Sue Crosby and Laura Dobbins

References
Author sites providing marketing tips, tools and other book publishing resources

Author Resources
Here is a list of our other books:
Available at Amazon

Francesca of Lost #ati on –
Romance Adventure and winner of five literary awards

The Cancer Club -
a crazy, sexy, inspirational novel of SURVIVAL
* Selected as a top-ten finalist in the Next Best Fiction Author Contest by Hampton Roads Publishing and Hierophant Publishing

The Adventures of Baylard Bear –
a Story about being DIFFERENT - Poynter Global Ebook Honorable Mention – Children's Fiction

Why is Pookie Stinky? For Ages 4 to 7 Years Old
(Book One: "Silly" Puppy Series 1) - Short Picture Book Written in Rhyme

Sell more Ebooks –
How to increase sales and Amazon rankings using Kindle Direct Publishing
* Poynter Global Ebook First Place Winner – Marketing and Advertising

Advanced Kindle Book Marketing: How to Sell more Ebooks online with new Amazon promotions and Kindle Bestseller Tips –
Kindle Bestseller

#OTE:

All links are included on the Kindle Version or email kindlebookpromos@gmail.com and I will send you a PDF copy with the links.

Author Associations:

Alliance of Independent Authors
American Book Sellers Association
Author Marketing Club
Independent Book Publishers Association

Author Tools:

Book Descriptions that Sell (Free Ebook)
http://authormarketingclub.com/members/free-ebook-signup/

Book Description tools
   https://www.tckpublishing.com/how-to-use-html-to-format-kdp-kindle-
book-descriptions/

ISBN
http://www.isbn-us.com/

Design Services:

Author Marketing Club
Members are offered an array of author tools including a large selection of predesigned book covers

Book Market
John Kremer, book marketing expert and bestselling author, has an extensive list of artists at his website.

Foster Covers
George Foster, an award-winning designer known for many bestselling covers including Chicken Soup for the Women's Soul.

SPAWN
The Small Publishers, Artists and Writers Network (SPAWN) offers a $100 book design discount to its members.

But if you need to or wish to design the covers yourself, look for royalty-free art or pay someone up front for their photos or graphics. It's less complicated to buy these components outright so you don't have to deal with copyright or use issues later on.

Free and Paid Photo service:

Dreamstime
Flickr
Getty Photos.
Stock Xchange

Ebook Formatting Service:

Amazon provides a long list of ebook converting services:

Amnet
Booknook.biz
Codemantra
CreateSpace
Digital Divide Data

Fiverr is a great service to seek professional help for $5 but don't just hire the first service you find.
Formax Innodata Lapiz Newgen
Online Convert

Hybrid Publishers
Archway Publishing
Christopher Matthews Publishing
DiversionBooks
Entangled Publishing
MillCity Press
She Writes Press
Soaring Eagle Books

Print On Demand
Createspace
IngramSpark
Kindle Direct Publishing
Kobo Book Hub
Lightning Source
Nook and Kobo
Nook Boards
Nook Lovers
OverDrive
Smashwords
Story Finds

Web Hosting:
GoDaddy
Hostgator
Here is a consumer list of top 10 Web Host sites
http://bit.ly/2k4tavL

Here is a consumer list of top 10 Free Web Host sites
http://bit.ly/2llBDAb

Website Design

Here is a consumer list of top 5 Website Designing sites
http://top5-websitebuilders.com/

Websites for Authors:

Book Baby Blog
Digital Book Today
Digital Book World
Kindle Book Promos
Publishers Weekly
She Writes Press
The Author Marketing Club
The Kindle Book Review
Writer's Digest
Writers Weekly

Marketing Services

Amazon Programs that Help Promote Books

Amazon Advantage – This forum works best for small press publishers or book vendors needing distribution and warehousing at reasonable rates.

Audio – ACX is a program offered through Amazon that allows you to produce a digital audiobook version of your book which is integrated with the new Whispersync for Voice on Kindle. The product is a professionally-narrated work.

Author Central – This section is like a mini-blog at Amazon. Take advantage of this section with good content, images, interesting tidbits about you and your books. You can also add social media links and book appearance information here.

KDP Select – This is Amazon's Digital Book Platform and probably the most beneficial for authors. With KDP Select, you can use your book titles, descriptions, categories and keywords to make your book more visible. KDP Select also offers authors free book promotion days and enrollment in the Kindle Lending Library – two programs that give writers visibility and profits.

Look Inside the Book – this allows customers to skim a portion of your book before deciding on the purchase. Take advantage of this feature by offering enticing text at the start of your work – this means going against the grain of traditional publishing that sets credits, dedications, copyright and table of contents at the front of a book.

Amazon has also added three new programs:
Kindle Countdown Deal, Kindle Matchbook and Kindle Prime Membership.

Author Programs We Recommend

American Authors and Publishers Guild – This is a new membership site that assists independent authors with special sales and publishing needs.

Association of Publishers for Special Sales – Membership is $89 a year but you get a list of publishers seeking new work. You'll also receive free marketing tips and access to numerous experts in the business like book distributors, buyers and marketers. As a member you're eligible for large discounts regarding anything to do with publishing.

Brian Jud – Probably the #1 expert in this field. You can sign up for his services at Book Marketing Works. Brian also offers Book Marketing consultation to any author. If you tell him Laura Dobbins sent you, he will give you a discount but be sure to ask for it before paying.

New Shelves Distribution – Tell them Laura Dobbins sent you. This group specializes in sales to libraries, retailers and specialty shops.

TCK – Owned and operated by Tom Corson-Knowles, a respected bestselling author and book marketing expert. His company is an international publisher specializing in ebooks on Amazon Kindle.

The Cadence Group – Can help you with book packaging needs and sound advice on how to make your book sellable to retail store buyers. Best of all, they'll tell you when not to change a thing.

#ote : Some of these services are expensive with payment often required in advance. We are not their affiliates and will make no profit from your purchase. It should be noted, we only recommend people or services we have used ourselves. Keep in mind THERE ARE NO

GUARANTEED BOOK SALES. However, if you are willing to invest some time, money and equity sweat, if you are willing to learn and grow with the industry, you can be a bestseller.

Blog Tours
Bewitching Book Tours – A good place for Romance books.

Enchanted Book Promotions – Offers several tour options at affordable prices
.

Expresso Book Tours – Has a large following, including nearly 3,000 members on Goodreads. Tours usually include 15 blog stops. Prices are reasonable.

Goddess Fish Promotions – Book in advance as this is a popular site with several opportunities to promote your titles.

Orangeberry Book Tours – Has been in the business over 10 years and excels in site management.

Reading Addiction Virtual Book Tours – Very affordable prices for authors.
Sage Book Tours – Author owned and operated. One of our faves!

Book Reviews
Big-name Paid Review Sites:

Blue Ink Review - $395 and up
ForeWord Reviews – Clarion Reviews start at $335 and take up to 8 weeks
Kirkus Reviews – Start at $425 and takes up to 9 weeks. Other services available
Your First Review - $149 and includes a 7 point report

Other Paid Review Sites:

Book Review Buzz – For $25, you can list your book at this site and your title will be sent to a list of 1,700 readers. If you want a guaranteed book review, the fee is $150.

Kindle Book Review – This site offers very affordable prices for book review packages including a premium service that includes the purchase your book to help with sales rankings.
Portland Book Review – You do not have to be from San Francisco to submit your book for review. It is free to submit and be considered. For a fee, you are guaranteed a review.

San Francisco Book Review – You do not have to be from San Francisco to submit your book for review. It is free to submit and be considered. For a fee, you are guaranteed a review.

Verified Book Reviews – This is a paid review service that includes buying your digital book copies, a sale that will boost your rankings. In addition, the review will be listed as a verified buyer on Amazon.

Free Book Review Sites

Midwest Book Review – Run by good people. There is no charge for print editions and this organization makes its reviews available to libraries.

Kindle Obsessed – Could take up to 3 months for a review but it is free.

The Kindle Book Review – Has a list of reviewers and there is no charge.

The Author Marketing Club – You have to be a member to use the forums on this site, including the book review discussions, but it is free to sign up. In addition, premium members will also receive book marketing tools and instructions.

World Literary Café – You have to be a member but signup is free. This site offers a lot of forums over and above book reviews. In addition, there are a number of free and paid book marketing opportunities including tweet teams. Goodreads – Recently acquired by Amazon, it is still one of the largest author and reader connected communities online. There are a number of groups that discuss books, review threads and review request forums.

Book Blogger Directory – This site offers a large data base listed in alphabetical order of book bloggers that accept review requests.

BookReviews – This is a relatively new site with book review opportunities and includes an Author Pitch page where writers get 35 words or less to tell readers why they should buy a book.

How to Use Pinterest

The Book Designer
Pinterest
Your Writer Platform

Paid Publicity Sites

Booktastik Ebook Soda
Ereaders News

Twitter Tools

Hootsuite – This is an easy setup for beginners and the basic services are free. We use this when promoting our free day or discounted books. It allows you to set up multiple tweets and to schedule them in advance.

http://tinyurl.com/

https://bitly.com/

Socialoomph – This is perhaps the best known service and has evolved into a multi-tasking twitter operation. If you are a beginner, this site may be confusing or overwhelming but you can explore and test its benefits for free. Advanced users can purchase a professional setup with additional features. Two of the most popular benefits of this site are that you can set up a welcome message to your twitter followers and you can schedule tweets in advance.

Twitter Teams

Goodreads
The Author Marketing Club
Triberr
World Literary Café

Our sites on Twitter and Facebook

@99KindlePromos
@EbookCountdown
@freebookpromos
@penabook
EbookPromos

Where to List Free Book Promotions
(Most sites are for Amazon Books but many will also post Smashwords and Kobe listings)

Facebook Listing Sites:

Amazon Kindle
Bargain Ebook Hunter
Book Club Girl
Book Goodies
Book Lovers Haven
Book Riot
Canada Kindle Books
Digital Book Today
Ebook Promos
Ebooks FreeFreeFree
Free Book Club
Free Book Feed
Free Book Today
Free Books
Free Kindle Books
Free Today on Amazon
FreeBooksy - (Has a list of other Free Book Listing Sites)
Galley Cats
iAuthor
Indie Book Lounge
Indie Books List
Kindle Bestseller List
Kindle Obsessed
Mobile Read
New Free Kindle Books
One Hundred Free Books
Promote kdBook Free

Story Finds
The Kindle Book Review
UK Book Lovers
We Love Books
World Literary Cafe

Free Listing Sites:

Addicted to eBooks
Ask David
Author Marketing Club
Awesome Gang
Bargain Booksy
Bargain eBook Hunter
Book Barbarian – SciFi and Fantasy
Book Bear
Book Bongo
BookBub
Book Goodies
Book Gorilla
Book of the Day
BookSliced
BookStar
Book Swag
Booktastik
Digital Book Today
Daily Cheap Reads
Ebooksforfreeinc
eBook Lister
eBook Soda
eBook Stage
Ereader News Today

Flurries Unlimited
Free Book Dude
Free Booksy
Free eBooks Daily
Free Kindle Books and Tips
Frugal Freebies
Good Kindles
InkArcade
Indie Book Lounge
Indies Unlimited
justkindlebooks
Kindle Boards
Kindle Book Promos
Kindle Book Review
Kindle Nation Daily
Masquerade Crew
My Book Cave
PeopleReads
Pixel Scroll
Planet eBooks (US & UK)
Read Freely
Reading Deals
Ripley's Booklist – Young Adult Books
Steamy Romance Stories (Romance)
The Books Machine
The Choosy Bookworm
The Digital Ink Spot
The Ereader Cafe
The Fussy Librarian
World Literary Cafe

Paid Free Promo Listing Sites:
Kindle Book Promos
BookBub
Book Butterfly
Book Gorilla
Book Kitty
Book Sends
Book Tweeting Service
Digital Book Today
Ereaders News
Free Kindle Books and Tips
Just Kindle Books
Kindle Boards
The Kindle Book Review
One Hundred Free Books
Your Book Promoter

Twitter sites to post your Free Days:
@bookbub
@Booksontheknob
@Bookyrnextread
@CheapKindleDly
@DigitalBkToday
@digitalinktoday
@fkbt
@free
@freebookclub1
@freebookdude
@Freebookdeal
@freebookpromos
@freeebooksdaily
@freebooksy

@freedailybooks
@4FreeKindleBook
@free_kindle
@FreeKindleStuff
@FreeReadFeed
@free2kindle
@IndAuthorSucess
@IndieKindle
@ibdbookoftheday
@KindleBookBlast
@KindleBookKing
@Kindlbookreview
@KindleDaily
@KindleEbooksUK
@kindlenews
@kindle_free
@Kindlefreebies
@KindleFreeBook
@kindlefreebooks
@kindle_mojo
@Kindle_promo
@kindlestuff
@KindleUpdates
@penabook
@pixelofink
@WLCPromotions
@zilchebooks

Where to List .99 Book Deals
(Most sites are for Amazon Books but many will also
post Smashwords and Kobe listings)

Awesome Gang

Bargain Booksy – Not as pricey as Bookbub but more costly than other sites. Still, a nice platform for promoting.

Bargain eBook Hunter
Bibliotastic
Book Daily
Book Deal Hunter
Book Goodies
Bookbear

BookBub – on the pricey side – and you must be pre-approved. But if you have the right type of book, big sales are possible.
Books Butterfly
Buck Books
Daily Free ebooks – Don't let the site name fool you! This forum is no longer a free ebook promotion service; it's dedicated to books costing 99 cents or less.
Ebook Stage
Ereader News Today
Fire and Ice Book Tours
Free Discounted Books
Get Free Ebooks
GoodKindles
Just Kindle Books
Kindle Book Promos – free and paid promotions available.
Kindle Nation Daily
Kufads

Many Books
Obooko
Read Cheaply
Spoiled Reader
Steamy Romance Books
StoryFinds
The Fussy Librarian
The Independent Author Network
The Kindle Book Review
The Wall of Books
The Women's Nest
Zwoodle Books

Good Twitter Sites:

https://twitter.com/ebooks99cents
https://twitter.com/99KindlePromos
https://twitter.com/99ebooks
https://twitter.com/KindleSwag
https://twitter.com/CrazyKindle
https://twitter.com/99centsale
https://twitter.com/book_tribe
https://twitter.com/AllKindleDeals

Kindle Book Promo Sites

Book Goodies
Books Machine
Digital Ink Today
Digital Book Today
E-Reader News
Kindle Book Promos
World Literary Cafe

Good FACEBOOK sites to list your promos:

Ebookpromos
KindleCountdownDeals
Kindle Countdown and $.99 Deals
Ereader News Today

Twitter:

@EbookCountdown
@KindleDailyDeal
@kindledeals
@freebookpromos
@CrazyKindle
@AllKindleDeals
@KindleDeals_
@ShopKindleDeals

About the Authors

Lucinda Sue Crosby is a multi-award-winning author, journalist and environmentalist. She is a Nashville songwriter, commissioned poet and lecturer. To learn more about the author, visit her Author Page: www.luckycinda.com

Laura Dobbins is a former newspaper reporter, page designer and editor. She has won numerous writing awards as an author and journalist. She also operates Kindle Book Promos, a site dedicated to promoting authors and their work.
http://kindlebookpromos.luckycinda.com

www.ingramcontent.com/pod-product-compliance
Lightning Source LLC
Chambersburg PA
CBHW052053270326
41931CB00012B/2743